KU-680-649

Introduction

With its soft, velvety fur, charming little black-button eyes, its minuscule stump of a tail and its short, stocky body, the hamster is, an extremely desirable domestic pet. In addition, hamsters possess a number of advantages compared with larger pets.

- They are eminently suitable for the novice pet-keeper.
- They are inexpensive to buy.
- They do not take up a lot of space and do not need much food.

By caring for a pet like a hamster, children as well as adults will learn how to handle living creatures carefully and, above all, to assume responsibility for them.

Discussed in this book are the four different species of hamster that are more or less available in pet-stores. The advice given is generally applicable to all these species and any differences in their keeping or care are mentioned separately.

The best-known species is the **Syrian**, or **golden, hamster** (*Mesocricetus auratus*). The other three species available are smaller hamsters. The **Chinese**, or **striped, hamster** (*Cricetulus griseus*) has been available as a pet for about 15–20 years. **Russian (Djungarian) dwarf hamsters** (*Phodopus sungoris*) – including **Campbell's dwarf hamster** (*P. s. campbelli*) and the **'Winter White' dwarf hamster** (*P. s. sungoris*) – have become very popular in recent years.The smallest hamster, is **Roborovski's dwarf hamster** (*Phodopus roborovskii*) and this is also becoming increasingly available. It often moves much more quickly than other hamsters, and is, therefore, not quite as ideal as a pet for stroking

Things to consider beforehand

You should always consider very carefully your desire to keep a pet, as the initial enthusiasm over a newly acquired pet very often wanes rather quickly, even in so-called animal-lovers, and the pet is then given only the most basic care, if any at all. Hamsters are relatively short-lived and not very demanding, but they do have a few needs that should be considered.

The following questions are intended to help you in making your decision.

- Are you prepared to accept that hamsters, with a few exceptions, are active at dusk and at night? Disturbances during the daytime mean stress for a hamster that could result in a shortened life-span.

Opposite: *The world looks quite different when standing on your head. Will this hamster be able to get down again safely?*

- Do you have enough room for a cage? Keeping a hamster in your bedroom will almost definitely disturb your sleep. Positioning the cage in the kitchen, a draughty front room or a smoky living-room will not be good for your pet's health. Remember that hamsters are rodents and may create dust and leave bite-marks.
- Are all the members of your family agreeable to keeping the new pet?
- Are you or any of your family allergic to dust or fur?
- Do you know anyone – a friend or relative – who can take care of your hamster during your holidays? Theoretically it is relatively easy to take a small pet on holiday with you if you are taking a car but the amount of stress to which the creature will be subjected – heat, cold, noise, draughts – will often prove harmful. You can simply take your pet, in its quarters, to your friend,

Like nearly all mammals, Syrian hamsters have lighter coloured bellies.

Previous pages: Left: An albino Syrian hamster with one full pouch. Right: A wild-coloured Syrian hamster.

5

together with sufficient food and bedding to last during absence.
- Many hamsters are tame enough to be held in the hand but even a tame animal may occasionally bite, either 'accidentally' or in self-defence. Would this be a reason for not acquiring a hamster as a pet?

A hamster as a present?

As already mentioned, a sense of responsibility can be encouraged through the task of caring for another creature. This is why it can be a good idea to allow children and young people to grow up with animals. Children between 1 and 8 years old should be helped and supported by adults when caring for animals and they should always wash their hands immediately after handling them.

Even if hamsters are skilful climbers, falling from a great height can be dangerous.

As the acquisition of a hamster should be well thought through beforehand, it is stupid or, at worst, cruelty to animals to give someone a surprise present of a hamster.

The right kind of cage

In addition to the usual cages with bars that are obtainable in almost every pet-store, you can also house a hamster in a glass or plastic tank, or in a home-made cage. A number of different types of cage are available, or you could build one yourself.

Cages with bars

Wire cages with a plastic tray for a floor are purpose-built and are the most commonly used. However, many hamster cages on the market are either too small or have a barred floor which is quite

A hamster cage should ideally have a floor area of 50 × 40 cm (20 ×16 in) and a height of 25 cm (10 in). The equipment inside consists of a sleeping house, a climbing tree and an exercise wheel.

unsuitable for hamsters, which, as desert-dwellers, have short feet. Also the bars are often too far apart, especially for dwarf hamsters, which may escape as a result.

The following points should be considered when purchasing a cage for your hamster:

- The **minimum length** should be about 50–60 cm (20–24 in).
- The **space between the bars** should be no more than **10 mm** (**$^1/_2$ in**) for Syrian hamsters and no more than **5–6 mm (about $^1/_4$ in)** for dwarf hamsters.
- The **floor** should not consist of bars and if there is a second floor in the cage it should be made of plastic or wood.
- The cage should definitely have **horizontal bars**, as Syrian hamsters and Chinese hamsters love to climb and are very good at it. There are certain serious disadvantages in using birdcages for keeping hamsters, not least the fact that the door may not be strong enough to prevent them from escaping.

Glass tanks

Glass or plastic tanks are more suitable than barred cages for keeping little Roborovski's and Russian dwarf hamsters. These small hamsters hardly climb at all and will not need the bars. Glass **aquariums** and **terrariums**, with sliding front panels and ventilation hoods as necessary, can also be used.

In the case of aquariums that are open at the top, you should make sure that the height of the tank is no greater than the width.

Hamsters are ever-curious and love to investigate new objects.

Chinese and Syrian hamsters require plenty of climbing facilities in a glass terrarium. Another important item is the wire-covered lid.

In a tall, narrow aquarium, condensation from respiration and perspiration will become trapped and may encourage the growth of bacteria and fungi because the air in the tank will not be able to circulate freely.

A frame with wire mesh can be used to cover the aquarium and keep the hamsters safe from other pets, such as cats, which might otherwise harm them. This will not be absolutely necessary in the case of Roborovski's, Campbell's or Russian dwarf hamsters. Suitable terrariums, designed for reptiles, are available on the market but you will need to make sure that the ventilation grids (on the side or on top) and the runners for any sliding panels are made of materials that cannot be gnawed. It is, of course, possible to keep Chinese or Syrian hamsters in glass tanks.

In the wild, a Syrian hamster will build its nest at the end of a 2.4 m (8 ft) deep burrow, where it will create a 'camp' made of vegetable matter.

A large floor area relative to the size of the container will make up for the lack of climbing facilities. The recommended dimensions (length × width × height) for Roborovski's and Russian dwarf hamsters are 50 × 30 × 25–30 cm (20 × 12 × 10–12 in). The container should be a little larger for Syrian hamsters – 80 × 40 × 30–40 cm (32 × 16 × 12–16 in) – and, for Chinese hamsters, it should be 50–60 × 40 × 30–40 cm (20–24 × 16 × 12–16 in).

Syrian hamsters in particular must be housed on their own but small colonies of hamsters that get on together should, of course, be housed in larger containers. The sizes above are those recommended for one or two animals.

Of course, a container like this can never be too large – the limits are really only determined by the amount of space that you have available for your hamster.

Building your own hamster cage

It is not very difficult to build a hamster home with a few do-it-yourself skills, although you must be careful to ensure that your hamster will not be able to gnaw its way out. Coated chipboard approximately 12–15 mm (about 1/2 in) thick can be screwed together to make a box. Avoid leaving any exposed ends or your pet will be tempted to gnaw at them.

If you wish, you can insert a pane of glass at the front and add a barred lid at the top, using zinc-coated iron mesh. Alternatively, with a bit of extra effort, you could build a type of hutch with a mesh door (resembling a wooden terrarium with a barred front wall).

Fix a strip of glass or wood about 15–20 cm (6–8 in) high along the bottom of the front wall to prevent litter being thrown out. Recommended sizes are given on p. 8.

Trust and curiosity shine out of this little fellow's eyes.

Where should the cage be kept?

The cage should be placed in a slightly **raised** position because hamsters, like many other rodents, react fairly strongly to 'danger from on high' (e.g. hawks) – even if it is the friendly hand of their carer.

Hamsters, in common with other small mammals, are sensitive to **noise** so the cage should **not** be positioned near loudspeakers, a radio or a television.

Avoid placing the cage near **curtains** – it is so easy for hamsters to demolish and chew up fabric for nesting material.

In and out: a wooden tube like this provides continuous variety.

Although many hamsters are desert-dwellers, they do not like **heat** in the form of direct sunlight or being close to a radiator. In the wild, they protect themselves from the heat of the sun by being active in the cool of the night and by retreating into deep underground burrows during the day.

Draughts, high humidity combined with low temperatures, and **cigarette smoke** are all likely to have adverse effects on a hamster's health.

Equipping the cage

Equipment in the cage – **sensible** equipment – is at least as important for your pets as the size of the cage.

The best type of **litter** is **wood shavings** sold specifically for use as small-animal bedding. These are relatively dust-free, very absorbent and light in weight, as well as being free of any toxic wood-preservatives. Sawdust from carpenter's workshops is not usually clean enough and is full of dust that may get into the hamster's eyes.

Even a clay flowerpot can provide an excellent hiding place.

Fine, dry **sand** offered for birds and chinchillas can also be used for Russian, Campbell's and Roborovski's dwarf hamsters. The disadvantage is that it does not absorb moisture very well and, being much heavier, may be difficult to dispose of. As soil often contains parasites or germs, its use as litter is not recommended. Peat should not be used for conservation reasons; it may also stain your pet's fur. Soil or clay can only be used for building burrows if it is moist and, in any event, it is thoroughly unsuitable for hamsters which love dry conditions.

Only very young hamsters like physical contact when they are sleeping.

The variety of hamster houses knows no bounds! A little house like this would be better standing on the ground.

Syrian hamsters can climb well but are not quite as flexible and agile as mice, for example. A fall from a height of 1.2 m (4 ft) onto a hard surface can be dangerous for a hamster.

Upside-down, unglazed **flowerpots** or clay bowls can serve as excellent hiding places for many species of rodent. Clay pots are cheap, easy to clean with hot water and have 'built-in ventilation' (the drainage hole). They can even be partly buried to create 'tunnels'.

For Syrian hamsters, use pots with a diameter of about 12–14 cm (4$^{1}/_{2}$–5$^{1}/_{2}$ in); for dwarf hamsters the diameter should be about 8–10 cm (3–4 in). For Syrian hamsters, carefully knock out a hole about 5 × 5 cm (2 × 2 in) in the side-wall of the pot; for dwarf hamsters the hole should be about 2 × 3 cm ($^{3}/_{4}$ × 1 in).

11

Using hamster 'wool' for nesting material needs a certain amount of care.

Alternatively you can simply arrange the pot so that the hamster can enter via the large end. Any sharp edges should be filed off a little. Once the pot is turned upside down, the hole will form an entrance.

Wooden **nesting boxes** for budgerigars are also very suitable for hamsters. The removable roof makes it easier to check the nest and the presence of a floor enables you to clean the cage without disturbing the Syrian-hamster nest. The entry hole of the nesting box should be slightly enlarged because pregnant females might otherwise have difficulty getting inside.

Most hamster 'houses' for sale in pet-stores are not very useful. They are often too small (particularly for Syrian hamsters), usually made of plastic or varnished wood and cannot be opened, so it becomes impossible to check the nest. Small splinters of plastic or bits of varnished wood may injure the animals' intestines or may even be toxic.

Many dwarf hamsters prefer to gather up litter in a corner of their cage to make a nest. In my experience, this is a very individual matter so it is best to experiment and see what your own hamster prefers.

The best **nesting materials** are **tissue paper** (toilet paper or unperfumed paper tissues cut into strips) and **hay**. Hamster 'wool' available from pet-stores should be used with care because your hamster's claws may get caught up in it.

Clean paper or cardboard boxes may also be given to hamsters. They provide material for the animals to gnaw and somewhere for them to hide. Hamsters will often use the chewed-up remnants as nesting material.

Always popular with Syrian hamsters. Below: Cardboard boxes for gnawing to pieces. Opposite: A treadmill wheel. Note: A solid wheel is preferable to one with rungs.

As most hamsters are very agile and may travel long distances in the wild, an **exercise wheel** will be very useful to enable them to get rid of their surplus energy although the Syrian-hamster wheels for sale in pet-stores are generally too large for Russian, Campbell's and Roborovski's dwarf hamsters. If the cage is large enough, a wheel will help to satisfy the hamster's urge to run. Buy an exercise wheel which is solid, rather than one with rungs, as your pet could otherwise get one of its feet trapped.

Metal exercise wheels can be obtained which are either free-standing or can be fixed to the side of the cage. In glass tanks

which have been adapted as hamster homes free-standing wheels will have to be used. Plastic wheels are more likely to be gnawed and so will soon have to be replaced.

A food-dish and a drinking-bottle.

Small **branches**, or pieces of **cork bark**, will provide hamsters living in glass tanks with an opportunity to climb but be sure that they will not enable the hamsters to escape.

Flat, firm-standing, ceramic or pottery **dishes** are best for juicy food or grain. Plastic dishes will, sooner or later, be gnawed but the provision of wood and other more natural options should divert your hamster's interest elsewhere.

While hamsters may get most of their liquid requirements from greenstuffs, they should still be provided with fresh drinking-water. Special **drinking-bottles** are available for this purpose. In the case of mesh cages, the drinking-bottle can be poked through from the outside. In glass tanks, either use suction pads to fix the drinking-bottle to the glass or, using silicon or other special glue, stick the bottle to the glass by its attachment. Some designs

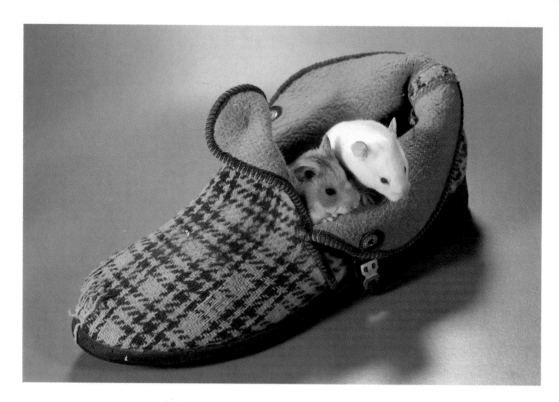

Attention is needed if you are going to let your hamster run around free in your home! A hide-away in a slipper is a relatively minor danger.

of drinking-bottles have wire loops by which they can be suspended from the top of the tank, within reach of the hamster.

Water-containers occasionally get buried in litter and any water running out may make the litter soggy; this is not beneficial to the health of hamsters, which originate from arid parts of the world. This is why it is not a good idea to provide drinking-water in open pots.

Choosing and buying a hamster

Syrian hamsters belong among those pets which are commonly stocked by most **pet-stores**. Dwarf hamsters, particularly the Russian ones, are also becoming increasingly available.

Other recommended ways of obtaining hamsters are through **advertisements** in animal magazines or periodicals, or from **friends** or **acquaintances** who breed rodents and would welcome some-one willing to take some of the offspring off their hands. If you are interested in exhibiting hamsters, then obtain stock from a **specialist breeder.**

How to recognize a healthy hamster

With careful observation and the help of the following checklist, you should be able to tell whether or not a hamster is healthy.

14

Running around free is not suitable for these Roborovski's dwarf hamsters; they are much too small and move about very quickly.

- The **fur** should be shiny and should not display any bald patches. Hamsters will lose their fur normally as they grow older, and such patches are often a sign of old age. There is not much that can be done to combat hair loss unless the cause is a parasitic infection, which may strike at any stage. Small scars on the tail or the edges of the ears are generally the marks of fights or biting.
- The **eyes** of the hamster should shine brightly and should not look at all crusty.
- The **anus** and the surrounding area should definitely not be dirty. Diarrhoea caused by infections or worms can result in a quick death.
- The **nose** should not look crusty or runny.
- Once woken up, hamsters should not lie about apathetically nor begin to run around frantically. These symptoms can, however, appear not only in animals that are sick but also in animals that are shut up in overcrowded trading cages. Never buy an animal because you are sorry for it because stressed hamsters of this kind are highly susceptible to disease. Roborovski's dwarf hamsters, which always begin to run around 'nervously' when disturbed, are the exception.

Buying animals out of pity will always benefit the seller rather than

A few more tips on choosing a hamster. Wild-coloured animals are considered to be the toughest, most long-lived and healthiest. Patched varieties are often nervous but may lose their nervousness with good care. Russian dwarf hamsters are particularly tame and look plump and comfortable with their interesting fur.

15

Hamsters do not always get on well together. This is a typical threat posture.

the animals. Some pet-sellers are pleased to be rid of animals that nobody wants and will not bother to treat others any better in the future. This will not change anything for the animals. Exceptions are hamsters with healed-up scars or mutilated tails which may be offered at a reduced price or for nothing. Hamsters like these will often attain a great age despite their disability.

One hamster or several?

Many people, being naturally sociable animals themselves, are incapable of imagining that there are animals which are voluntarily solitary or will (usually) act defensively if approached by a strange member of their own species.

Keeping a single hamster is not being cruel. In fact, it will create great stress and torment if you keep animals together that cannot 'stand' one another.

In the wild, Syrian hamsters are **solitary** creatures; only some dwarf hamsters will live in pairs. During recent years, selective breeding has produced hamsters that are more peaceable towards members of their own species but fighting can still break out unexpectedly. It has even become possible to keep several Syrian hamsters together under certain conditions but this is not to be recommended because of the inherent danger.

If you really want to keep two or more hamsters in one cage, you should obtain either young animals that will become accustomed to each other or litter siblings. In my own experience, it is the male animals that seem to get on better with each other. As the initial state of peace among young animals may not last for ever, you should be ready for 'emergencies' and provide any animals that may be bitten and chased away with some opportunity of retreating.

Russian and Roborovski's dwarf hamsters generally have fewer problems getting on with each other than Chinese or Syrian hamsters. In most cases, pairs or two adults of the same sex will also get on reasonably well.

A young hamster or an older one?

Hamsters, like most rodents, live for only a relatively short time, so I recommend obtaining young animals. At an age of at least 4 weeks, they can be removed from their mothers without harm. Contrary to prevailing opinion, even adult hamsters can become tame. One of the prettiest wild-coloured Syrian hamster males that I ever had was bought as an adult. Although it had grown up in a

Sexual features in Syrian and Chinese hamsters. Below left: a female. Below right: a male.

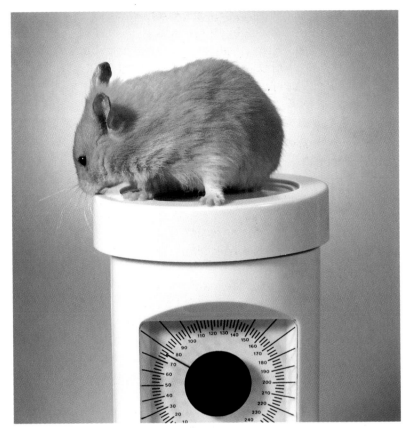

Little hamsters grow up extremely quickly. After 2 or 3 months they will have gained 30 times their birth weight.

To determine the sex of hamsters, pick up several animals by the scruff of the neck and they will spread their legs. This will enable you to check the distance between the genital opening and the anus which characterizes each sex. The shape of the hindquarters when viewed from the side can also help, being more elongated in males.

pet-store, it was completely tame from the first day onwards and was always very friendly towards other members of its species. This hamster's behaviour was almost certainly unusual but it goes to show that, even among animals that may look exactly the same, there may be great individual differences, as many of the young of this particular male were aggressive and unfriendly.

A male hamster or a female?

The question of which sex to buy is really only of importance if you are intending to keep several hamsters and if you want to breed from them. In Syrian hamsters and Chinese hamsters, it is usually the females which are the more aggressive, although, among these species in particular, more peaceable animals have now been bred for some years.

As many pet-store-keepers, and even some breeders, are not very good at sexing animals, here are some tips if you need to check:
- In Syrian and Chinese hamsters the males have paired testicles near the base of the tail. These are clearly visible – even in young

animals of 4 weeks onwards – and can be felt with the fingers.

- In females, the distance between the genital opening and the anus is noticeably smaller than in males.
- In Roborovski's and Russian dwarf hamsters, sexing is considerably more difficult as very often the testicles are not visible in the males. Here, you can only judge by the distance between the genital opening and the anus, which is significantly shorter in females. In mature animals a further distinction can be made, as the males have a more active gland on their belly, which makes the surrounding fur look moist.

A plastic container with a mesh lid like this is most suitable for transporting your hamster, provided that it is padded with hay and litter.

Transporting your hamster home safely

Carrying containers made of transparent plastic, with a barred lid and a couple of handles, are very suitable for transporting small rodents. If you buy a slightly larger box, you will have a spare cage from the start which can be used as temporary housing while the proper cage is being cleaned, or for individuals which have been bitten, or to house young animals. Plenty of litter, tissue and/or hay will prevent the hamsters from sliding about and injuring themselves. During a short journey, it will not be necessary to add food, as the little animals will not eat anyway, because of the stress of being moved.

It is important to keep the container upright and in a position out of sunlight because this will make the hamsters feel more secure. Naturally, you should shelter the container from unpleasant weather conditions, such as rain, heat, cold or wind. Cardboard or paper cartons supplied by pet-store-keepers will rarely stand up to the gnawing teeth of desperate Syrian hamsters for very long (5–15 minutes). This means that they could easily escape on the journey home. Only dwarf hamsters can be transported in such containers with no problems for any longer than this.

Opposite: With the help of delicacies like this, most hamsters can soon be persuaded that people are not dangerous.

Adjustment period

The stress of new smells and being moved irritates and disturbs most rodents so they will initially hide themselves. Hamsters are usually curious, however, and will soon begin to explore their new

The right grip is important when lifting a hamster.

Hamsters are used to orienting themselves by their sense of smell and to 'sniffing' danger.

Opposite: A tame hamster will happily climb from hand to hand.

home thoroughly, especially under cover of darkness. Give your new pet plenty of **time** and be very **patient** with it! Allow it a few days of peace. As understandable as your excitement, pride and curiosity may be at the beginning, please do not invite all your friends and neighbours around to see your new pet. Hamsters are, for the most part, active in darkness, and so all attempts at taming them should be concentrated on this active time, i.e. in the evening or at night. Hamsters live solitary lives and it will take them quite a while to make contact voluntarily with human beings. As is the case with many opportunist feeders, getting to know them will usually happen via their stomachs. Try using **delicacies** such as nuts, sunflower seeds or mealworms to entice your hamster from its lair. Hold your hand very still in the cage or terrarium and lay the titbit on the flat of your palm.

Your hamster will probably come out only after a great deal of hesitation and will then take the titbit back to its hiding place to eat it. It may happen that the little rodent will carefully try to nip your hand. Do not jump – easier said than done! – as it will lose its trust immediately. This very gentle 'nipping' will almost never break the skin and should be seen as careful probing or 'tasting'.

After a while, the hamster will become used to your hand as a food-dispenser and will realize that it represents no danger. As soon as your hamster begins to take food from your hand, you can very carefully try to hold it and pick it up. However, if it stands up on its back legs, clacks its teeth and hisses (defensive pose), it means your attempt at making contact was rather premature and you run the risk of getting a nasty bite.

As soon as your hamster has accepted your touch, you can gradually begin to cease offering it titbits as enticement. Once your hamster no longer displays signs of fear, you can try to pick it up for the first time. The right way to handle your hamster is described on p. 22.

Unfortunately, problems can arise again and again when trying to gain a hamster's trust. Hamsters, like many other rodents, are primarily olfactory animals, i.e. they rely primarily on their sense of smell to gain information while visual recognition plays a much lesser role than in primates and human beings. For this reason, you may find that a hamster suddenly wishes to defend itself against a familiar hand as soon as it smells of a different perfume, different soap or a different kind of food, and it may even bite as a result.

You should definitely consider the fact that there are vast differences between individual hamsters. In the case of more placid

20

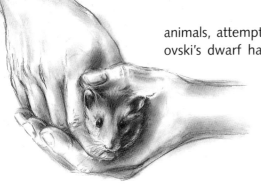

A hamster will feel quite secure in the hollow of your hands.

A hamster should be allowed peace and quiet during the day. Always wake it at the same time every evening if it does not wake up by itself. A Syrian hamster will be able to get used to its owner in this way and will leave its sleeping place at the sound of its name.

Opposite: *What can be hidden behind this brick?*

animals, attempts at taming will fall on more fertile soil. Roborovski's dwarf hamsters, which are naturally very active, can be superficially tamed only with a great deal of effort and patience.

How to handle your hamster

A tame hamster which does not mind being handled can be picked up around its middle with one hand and placed in the palm of the other hand. The two hands then form a kind of 'cave' where it will feel secure. Hamsters which are not quite tame, or restless Roborovski's dwarf hamsters, can thus be prevented from running away at any time.

As already mentioned above, Russian, Campbell's and Roborovski's dwarf hamsters all have no real concept of heights so they may occasionally fall, which could be dangerous. When they are allowed to run across a table top or a similar surface, they should be watched carefully. Picking up a hamster in a loose grip by the scruff of its neck has often been recommended but should only be adopted by very experienced pet-owners as it is very easy to injure the hamster or to be bitten.

Tame Syrian and Chinese hamsters that love climbing, and are good at it, can be allowed to climb up your clothes. The hamster may even try to climb under your shirt or blouse. As long as you are not ticklish, you can let them carry on. Many hamsters like the dark and the body warmth, but take care not to move suddenly or you may be scratched or bitten.

Should your hamster run free in the living-room?

The apparent freedom of the living-room actually presents more dangers to your hamster than advantages. It may seem to offer interest and plenty of variety to a hamster but the chances of your pet having an accident are, however, very great.

In addition, catching a hamster that is running around freely in the room is not as easy as you might think. Even a tame hamster may not voluntarily return to your hand and it can disappear, e.g. behind furniture, where it may be hard to reach.

Avoid creating stress for your hamster by giving it this imagined pleasure, and do not allow dwarf hamsters in particular to run about in a room. A cage equipped with plenty of objects offering variety will generally guarantee them a longer life than a couple of hours of 'freedom' a day.

If you really believe that they need to get out, Syrian hamsters can be allowed to run around the room provided that great care is taken and they are kept under constant observation. The greatest danger lies in underestimating their climbing abilities. Innumerable hamsters, while trying to get down again from a curtain pole or tall cupboard which they had swarmed up with the 'chimney-climbing technique', have plunged to the ground. Hamsters love climbing upwards but are quite clumsy when it comes to climbing down again. In most cases they just let themselves drop, which can easily result in fatal spinal injuries.

Hamsters also love to climb into cracks and may get stuck. Many tall wall-cupboards have a gap between the back and the wall – often not that visible to the owner. The hamster may fall into the gap from above and then can only be rescued if the cupboard is pulled as far away as possible from the wall. The following points should also be considered when allowing a hamster to run free:

These small, fast-moving dwarf hamsters can be picked up easily in a cardboard tube.

- All **electric wires** and **cables** and electrical outlets, in particular, should be inaccessible to a hamster.

Everything needs to be checked out!

- All **water-filled containers**, e.g. vases, basins and aquariums, should be covered securely.
- All dangerous or toxic **indoor plants**, e.g. poinsettias, cacti,

mother-in-law's tongue and ivies, should be removed.

- All **textiles,** e.g. carpets, fabric wallpapers and upholstery, should be watched carefully. Hamsters just love to utilize pieces of fabric for lining their nests and may cause damage accordingly.
- Take care with **dogs** and **cats**! Only very rarely are they so peaceable and their hunting instinct so subdued that they will get on with a hamster.
- Check before you **sit down** and where you are **treading.** Many hamsters have been accidentally squashed by their owners in this way.

You may prefer to build an exercise area in the form of a mesh-covered wooden framework, which is likely to be safer for your hamster.

Just like the entry to an underground burrow!

A titbit inside a cardboard tube ... the easy way to catch an escaped hamster!

What to do if your hamster escapes

Should your hamster manage to escape from its cage unnoticed, first try to find out in which room your pet may be. This can be established through evidence of gnawing, or rustling and scratching

Another way to catch an escaped hamster.

noises at night. A piece of apple or other food will be useful during the search; missing or nibbled food will indicate in which room the fugitive may be, helping you to track down your pet.

If your hamster has escaped at night, it will be rolled up and fast asleep during the day. Check all cracks and gaps between furniture. Check all upholstered furniture, particularly underneath. Move it very carefully, to reduce any risk of injury to your pet.

If your search remains fruitless but you have a good idea in which room your hamster may be, place its shelter – without the nesting material – somewhere near a wall. A few **cardboard tubes** will offer further places to hide in.

With any luck, on the following morning you will find your hamster sleeping peacefully in one of the hideouts you have placed ready. If your search still remains unsuccessful, however, stand a **tall container,** laden with food, titbits and some nesting material to serve as bait, in the room. Rest a thin piece of wood or similar item against the rim to provide a 'ladder'. The aim is for the hamster to smell the food, climb up the wood and fall into the container.

If you leave the cage open, in the hope that it will return voluntarily, keep watching it. Your hamster may merely move its food and nesting material from its old home to another locality elsewhere.

A hamster that has escaped and reached the outside world has very little chance of survival. Cars, dogs, cats and birds of prey will not allow it to live for long.

Care during your holidays

This time for people to recover and relax is usually associated with stress and discomfort for pets. The worst possible solution for both parties would be to set a hamster free in what seems to be a favourable spot. These pampered little pets are no longer geared-up to a life in the wild and would soon fall victim to predators. Furthermore, it is generally prohibited by law to abandon animals that are not native to a country.

Opposite: Above: Here a hamster's cheek-pouches are just the thing for storing and carrying food. Below: This is how the collected food is stroked out of a hamster's cheeks.

Should you wish to take your hamster on holiday with you, make absolutely sure beforehand that your pet will be welcome in your holiday quarters. Place it in a well-padded container during any car journey. If possible, take its usual cage with you. Avoid draughts, heat, cold and exposure to intense sunlight. Your hamster should be

no worse off than it would be at home while you are having a good time. Never leave your pet alone in a car, as the temperature inside could rise to a fatal level on a hot day. Also, do not transport a hamster in the boot (trunk) because of the risk of exhaust fumes.

It is a much better idea to hand over your pet to relatives, friends or a pet-store to be cared for during your absence. These little pets are easy to look after and will not create a lot of work for 'holiday carers'.

If you are only going away for a couple of days, there may be no problem about leaving your hamster alone but you should still arrange for someone to check on your pet every day. Leave your pet with enough grain and long-lasting juicy vegetables, such as carrots You can also leave a drinking-bottle as a reserve.

Opposite: *Grains and seeds with a fat content that is not too high are the basic food for hamsters.*

The right foods for your hamster

Most species of hamster are desert- or steppe-dwellers. In these environments there is an abundant supply of food for short periods of time but only very little for the rest of the year. A hamster's cheek-pouches serve to transport considerable quantities of food and this has enabled hamsters to adapt to the situation in the wild. Food is collected while it is available and hoarded underground for use during the rest of the year. When choosing food, you should consider the way in which hamsters live in the wild. Fibre-rich and, on the whole, low-fat food is particularly suitable for the desert dwelling Roborovski's and Russian dwarf hamsters.

To prevent symptoms of deficiency, you should to try to offer a varied diet. Different types of **grain** will cover the carbohydrate requirements and will provide fibre. **Fruit** and **vegetables** will also provide the creatures with fluids and vitamins. **Animal protein** is a vital building block for making tissue. Food left over from the dining-table is harmful to hamsters as they cannot cope with salt, spices and fat. Very sweet things are extremely popular – as with people – but they are not healthy. Contrary to popular opinion, animals do not always know what is good for them and will even eat food that is potentially harmful.

Seed-cakes or pellets among its food ensure that a hamster's teeth are worn down adequately.

Grain

The natural diet consists primarily of seed. Grain is usually rich in carbohydrates and is therefore recommended as a basic food.

In my experience, the hamster **food mixtures** available are not very popular with the animals themselves. If you are keeping dwarf hamsters, you will not be able to do much with this food as most of the constituents are too large for these smaller hamsters. It is much cheaper and better to mix your own food.

For Syrian hamsters, use guinea-pig food mixed with about 20 per cent budgerigar food and about 10 per cent canary food and give them dog flakes that have meat and vegetable components as an additional source of proteins and vitamins.

For dwarf hamsters, the proportion of fine grains should definitely be higher:
- Russian and Roborovski's dwarf hamsters should receive about 40 per cent budgerigar food, 40 per cent canary food, 10 per cent guinea-pig food and 10 per cent dog flakes.
- Chinese hamsters should be given 30 per cent budgerigar food, 30 per cent canary food, 30 per cent guinea-pig food and 10 per cent dog flakes.

28

Plenty of variety in the diet and nibbling-sticks to wear down the teeth are prerequisites for a healthy life.

Opposite: *These items also belong on a hamster's menu: moisture-rich cucumbers as a substitute for drinking-water, and most important, lettuce, fruit and nuts.*

Check that the guinea-pig food does not have too many fatty components. **Peanuts** and **sunflower seeds** are very popular but can cause your pet to put on weight and upset the intestines, which are specialized to deal with low-fat food.

Grain can be replaced by well-dried, non-mouldy **bread**, **crispbread** and **oats**. Small pressed cakes and special pellets should be offered to breeding hamsters. They contain everything necessary apart from water but form a rather monotonous diet.

Nibbling-sticks, sold in pet-stores, come in different flavours and are quite good food value, as well as keeping your pet occupied, but they are relatively expensive.

Greenfood and juicy food

Rather than drinking to obtain their liquid requirements, hamsters will often prefer to eat juicy food. A wide range of different fruits and vegetables can be used to provide a good supply of vitamins – and best of all are those picked fresh from your own garden.

Vegetables and saladstuffs

An adequate vitamin content in food is very important. Necessary vitamins can be found in, e.g. dandelions and wheatgerm.

Carrots, **celery**, **beetroot**, **cucumbers**, **maize** and **courgettes** are recommended. You may also give your hamster small quantities of endive, iceberg and lamb's **lettuces**. I hesitate to recommend round lettuce because it is more often contaminated with pesticides than other types of lettuce. Avoid flatulence-producing vegetables, such as onions, cabbage and leeks.

Wash the vegetables thoroughly first with lukewarm water and dry them before giving them to your hamster.

Fruit

Pieces of **apple**, firm **pears**, **bananas** and very small quantities of **berries**, e.g. raspberries, strawberries or grapes, are also suitable.

Do not give hamsters very acidic fruit, e.g. oranges and kiwi fruit (Chinese gooseberries), as such fruits are very indigestible for small rodents.

Animal protein

It is very important to provide a source of protein because hamsters are not entirely herbivorous.

Research done in the wild on Roborovksi's dwarf hamsters has shown that these rodents eat up to 60–80 per cent protein at certain times. This high level of protein is not necessary when they are kept in captivity but it does prove that many supposedly

Opposite: *Irresistible!*
As you can see, this
little fellow has found
a delicious titbit.

vegetarian animals also eat sources of animal protein.

Dog biscuits, **chewing bones** and **beef bones** will serve as sources of protein and a means of gnawing. A small amount of **sour cream**, **yoghurt** or mild hard **cheese** is very popular and recommended. **Mealworms** and various **insects** that are offered as food for terrarium animals are also much favoured delicacies and an excellent source of protein. Pregnant and nursing females can also be given a little hard-boiled **egg yolk**. You should make sure that insects and perishable foods that will go off quickly are eaten immediately or else removed before they can cause harm.

Additional foods

Dwarf hamsters, in particular, will occasionally eat good-quality, dust-free **hay**. Sprays of **millet** offered for sale as bird food provide an ideal means of occupying your pet as well as additional food.

I always recommend **branches** and **twigs** of beech, birch, hazel and fruit trees for wearing down a hamster's teeth and for eating. You will be surprised how very sought-after these 'nibbling-sticks' are. Naturally, these twigs should be gathered far away from traffic fumes, sprays and sooty air; the leaves can then be utilized as well. Wash these off as an additional precaution.

Vitamins and minerals

With a sufficiently varied diet there will be no need for vitamin supplements, but I would still recommend sprinkling a vitamin and mineral mixture, in recommended doses, over the food every 2 or 3 days.

Vitamin supplements, as offered for human consumption, will be far too concentrated and an overdose will often have more harmful effects than giving too little. Special products intended for rodents are now available.

How much food will your hamster need?

It is almost impossible to give figures for the 'ideal' quantities of food, as consumption will depend on age, size and individual factors, such as level of exercise and the surrounding temperature. A properly balanced diet, with restricted amounts of fatty foods, is unlikely to result in a fat hamster, although hamsters may put on weight as they get older.

A sensible method which I practise is to give sufficient food (grain and juicy food) for a small amount to be left over the next day. Make sure too that your hamster does not bury a portion of

Large, open water-containers like this one are not recommended. They are easily knocked over or buried and will make the litter damp!

the food that it is given nor begin to create a store. You will realize after a while how much your hamster really needs.

As with all living creatures, there will be individual preferences – many a hamster will develop a passion for exactly the one food that another will totally reject. Always remember that balance in its diet is important.

Drinking-water

In the steppes and deserts of Asia, the native habitats of hamsters, there is very rarely any water to drink, so these creatures have to get all their liquid requirements mainly from the greenfood and roots that they eat.

A hamster's drinking-water requirements are difficult to estimate. It is, nevertheless, a good idea to offer it fresh water throughout the warm part of the year.

From my own experience I know that even pregnant and nursing hamsters can raise their young without any drinking-water. Even during these periods, their increased liquid requirements can usually be covered just by an adequate supply of juicy food (vegetables and fruit). Nevertheless you should still offer water.

Some breeders are now using only filtered water, or the still bottled waters sold for human consumption – because of fears that the levels of chlorine and heavy metals in mains drinking-water may be too high.

Regular tasks

- Among the necessary daily chores, are, firstly, **feeding** your hamster with grain and juicy food. Check the corners and hiding places in the cage as hamsters like to hide surplus food there.

- If **grain** is accumulated in this way, you should **check** it, because some hamsters, like other rodents, have a habit of marking their stores with urine. Mould will quickly start to grow on moist stores of seed. Do not give hamsters more food than they need each day.
- **Spoiled** food and juicy food or greenfood that has fallen into the litter should always be **removed.**
- **Clean** the **food-dishes** and **drinking-bottles** daily.
- **Remove** any large areas of **damp litter** about every 2 days from the corners where hamsters urinate. (Hamsters have special 'toilet' areas in their burrows in the wild.)
- Give the cage a **general clean-out** about **once a week**. This means removing the litter completely, replacing the nesting material if necessary and washing out the cage or glass tank with hot water and a non-toxic disinfectant.

For a change – a bit of a fight which need not always be very serious.

The frequency of general cleaning will also depend on the size of the cage, the number of animals, the manner of feeding and the species. Provided that you remove the damp litter regularly from the toilet areas, a really large cage will not have to be cleaned out quite so often. If the cage houses a number of hamsters, and if an excessive amount of fruits and vegetables is given, it will require more frequent cleaning out.

The cages of dwarf hamsters, which produce only very dry faeces if they are given the correct types of foods, will also not necessarily need cleaning out every week.

Do not employ strong-smelling or corrosive cleaning agents and never use any kind of air-freshener or room spray as they can all be dangerous to hamsters.

Facilities for gnawing and keeping your hamster occupied should be offered regularly and renewed. Often, the hamster will become bored with objects that have been lying about in its home for a long time.

Does your hamster need playthings?

As it is really only the young animals that 'play' in the human sense of the word, it is probably better to refer to 'occupation' rather than play. Hamsters in captivity do not have to look for food or expend much effort so they have more time for 'exploring' their surroundings. There are a number of ways of providing them with

Small twigs from fruit trees and hazel bushes are particularly popular playthings. They should not have been treated or sprayed.

stimulation in their cages. Social contact between hamsters living together is one sensible occupation, even though this is not really a species-connected activity, bearing in mind that most hamsters live a solitary life. Nevertheless 'playing' is a good substitute for hunting for food, an activity that is no longer necessary in a cage.

The provision of cardboard packaging and twigs helps to satisfy the urge to gnaw and provides plenty of activity. Toilet paper and cardboard tubes provide good hiding places, although they will often be demolished quite effortlessly with those little gnawing teeth. For a change, you can occasionally hide a few titbits or delicacies, or part of the food ration, inside a paper carton, underneath a heap of hay or in a screwed-up scrap of paper. In this way, the hamster will have to expend effort to get at its food. Feeding your pet in the evening and morning (juicy food at one meal, grain at the other) will stimulate activity. Do not stuff the hamster's nesting material into its hiding place for it, rather let it do it itself.

Various see-saws, swings, ladders and carousels offered in pet-stores may take up too much room for creatures that like to run about, unless their quarters are very large. 'Treadmill' wheels are very popular, seem to remain interesting for Syrian hamsters and do not need to be renewed frequently like other means of occupation. A large box filled with sand can help to satisfy their urge to burrow. You could also bury a few grains or seeds in the litter surface so that the hamster is stimulated to dig.

Breeding

You can gain a lot of enjoyment from watching young hamsters being raised by their mother. The desire to experience this can be one of the main reasons for wanting to breed these rodents.

Before proceeding to place a pair together for mating purposes, you should consider the following points carefully:

- Only breed hamsters if you are certain you will have enough room for all the youngsters. If you are planning regular litters of young you should make sure that you have a **firm commitment from a pet-seller** to take the young hamsters.

Courtship begins: a male and female sniffing at each other.

- Syrian hamsters and Chinese hamsters do not generally live peaceably with one another, and will probably not be able to stay together for very long, so you will need enough room for **other cages.** It may happen that the young cannot be accommodated somewhere else immediately so you should have other housing available for a short-term, temporary home. Russian and Roborovski's dwarf hamsters are, as a rule, much more placid. The male may remain with the female while she is raising the young.

- Even tame female hamsters should not be disturbed a great deal during pregnancy and while raising their young and they should be able to remain in their usual familiar surroundings. During the first 1 or 2 weeks after the birth, you should refrain from cleaning out the cage. This does mean you will be able to smell the hamsters (which are not normally very smelly). Some

Hamsters engaging in courtship games.

consideration and **tolerance** will be required. Dwarf hamsters are similarly sensitive to disturbances.

- Particularly during pregnancy and while nursing, hamsters have a higher protein requirement than normal. Make sure that they have an adequate supply of **protein-rich foods.**

Mating

Hamsters that do not normally get on well together should be put together only for mating purposes. As a rule,

A female offering herself for mating.

females that are not ready to mate will react aggressively and defensively towards other members of their own species.

The hormonally regulated readiness to mate (oestrus, when females are in season) occurs about every 4–7 days. Many female Syrian hamsters will display different behaviour during this time. They will be less defensive and, if touched on the rump or back, will raise their tails, offering themselves to the male for mating.

If you want the hamsters to mate, place the female into the male's cage. The male will feel more secure in his own cage and will be able to stand up to the female. If they do start fighting be prepared to separate them immediately as otherwise the male could suffer fatal injuries. Try putting them together on a daily basis until they mate successfully.

As soon as the female, who previously has been ready to defend herself, accepts the male, mating behaviour will begin. The male will chase the female and drive her in front of him. In between times, they will sniff at each other's genitals. After a while, and after repeated behaviour of this nature, the female will present herself to the male for mating with a hollowed back and erect tail. The actual mating will take only a few seconds. Both animals will then clean their genitals. As a rule, there will be repeated matings. After a while, the female's aggression will increase again and she will ward off her partner, who should be removed at this stage.

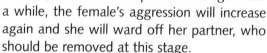

Mating hamsters.

Dwarf hamsters are more tranquil and the pair can be left together. Nevertheless, watch your hamsters carefully and separate them if there are serious fights.

Russian and Campbell's dwarf hamsters, and Chinese hamsters, can usually be kept in pairs or in small groups. (Naturally, the container for a dwarf-hamster colony should be larger than a cage for a solitary animal.)

Roborovski's dwarf hamsters should preferably be kept in pairs only for breeding purposes, although they may live in small groups at other times.

Pregnancy and birth

Syrian hamsters have one of the shortest gestation periods of all mammals. A few days before the birth, the female will begin some serious nest-building and gather together plenty of nesting

A peek into the nursery: most hamster mothers spend all day looking after their offspring. The centre of the world for 1–15-day-old hamster babies is mother's 'milk-bar'. Occasionally, the mother will transport her young fairly roughly.

material to 'upholster' her hiding place. Make sure to offer the expectant mother sufficient nesting material.

In cases where the male has not been driven away with bites, offer him a second place to sleep at this stage because the females of even the more tranquil species will not tolerate a male near the nest any longer. Because of the short gestation period, the young are very small at birth. Usually, they are produced with little fuss, one after the other, and, after being licked clean, begin suckling right away.

Young, inexperienced or shy hamsters may eat their young if they are disturbed. This kind of behaviour often provokes feelings

The original stock of most Syrian hamsters in captivity in the world today consisted of a female with 12 young, found in Syria in 1930. From these few specimens, various different breeds and colours have been raised during the past 50 years.

of disgust in human beings but the reasons are very natural. In an environment that is too insecure for offspring, there is more sense in re-using the nutrients (i.e. the young) and waiting for better times to produce more.

Growth and development of the young

Newborn hamsters are naked, blind and deaf – and so are totally helpless at birth. The mother's milk is the most important point of reference for the young during their first days of life. About 5 days after birth, you will notice the first traces of fluffy fur. At this same age, the young will already have begun to nibble at the food which their mother brings them. A few days after opening their eyes, the little hamsters will leave the nest for a first, brief 'exploration'. After about 14 days, their eyes will have opened. At this point, the mother will still spend a lot of time enthusiastically carrying her babies back to the nest.

For about 3 weeks – less in smaller litters – the young will continue to receive their mother's milk. After about 25 days, they will be completely independent of their mother and should then be separated from her because some hamsters start to become aggressive towards their young. Many dwarf hamsters, however, will accept their own young for a very long time, mostly for the rest of their lives.

Just 1 or 2 weeks after **weaning,** the young hamsters themselves may already be mature and ready to bear their own young. They should therefore be separated according to sex because very early pregnancies may have an adverse effect on the growth of females. Syrian hamsters take about 4–6 months to attain their maximum adult size.

Opposite: Colour variations among Syrian hamsters. Top left: An albino Syrian hamster. Top right: A Syrian hamster with reddish brown fur. Centre left: A black-and-white 'panda' Syrian hamster. Centre right: A cream-coloured Syrian hamster. Bottom left: A wild-coloured Syrian hamster. Bottom right: A patched Syrian hamster with long hair on its back.

Colour and fur varieties in hamsters

Several hundred generations of hamsters have been bred since the 'discovery' of the first living Syrian hamsters. The very close degree of relatedness of hamsters living in captivity (for a long time they were all descended from three or four siblings) has helped to encourage the development of mutations. This has resulted in a number of different colour and fur variations. It can be a fascinating business to breed for different colour and fur varieties. The rapid succession of generations means that results can be obtained in a fairly short time.

There are four different fur types in Syrian hamsters:
• Normal **short-haired** animals.

An alert, attentive expression.

If a hamster refuses its food, suddenly becomes unusually apathetic or loses weight, it should be watched carefully as these may be the first symptoms of illness.

- **Long-haired,** or **angora,** hamsters with warm, soft fur that needs lots of care; these are often called '**teddy**' hamsters, especially in North America.
- **Satin** hamsters with silky, shiny fur.
- **Rex** hamsters with slightly rough fur and curly whiskers.

A combination of these mutations is also possible so you can have, e.g., long-haired satin Syrian hamsters.

As with other animal species, there seems to be a connection between certain colours and types of behaviour. Hamsters that have dark fur or patches are often considered to be more aggressive than others.

In addition to the wild-coloured hamster, varieties include: **white** (with pink eyes), **black,** the particularly peaceable **cream** hamster and the **colour-point.** The colour-point is also called the '**Himalayan**' and is white with black eyes and apparently sooty-coloured ears, snout and feet. New colours are still being developed and some, like **silver** and **dark grey**, are only rarely seen for sale at present.

The **wild-coloured** variety of Syrian hamster, to my mind, is superior to all others. The vivid coloration on the back, the white belly and the dark stripes on the cheeks make it appear very colourful. Unfortunately, it is increasingly disappearing and many hamsters available now show less contrast in their coloration.

Patched hamsters come in all the colours mentioned above. Usually, the white patches are more or less irregularly shaped, although skilful breeding has resulted in symmetrical patching. So-called '**panda**' hamsters are often offered for sale; these are black with symmetrical, saddle-shaped white patches, resembling those of a panda.

Dwarf hamsters have not been kept in captivity for very long and have only been kept and bred in small numbers, so there are only a few variants with colours different from the natural ones. There are patched Chinese hamsters and white and patched Campbell's dwarf hamsters.

Russian dwarf hamsters which are kept in cool conditions during the winter may grow a different-coloured winter coat. It is very dense and almost snow-white, apart from the dark wavy line down the back. A satin mutation is known in this case as well.

The sick hamster

A hamster which is properly looked after will very rarely get sick. Many illnesses arise from, or are exacerbated by, receiving bad or wrong food or from being subjected to stress. For this reason, you should avoid all kinds of strain or stress, e.g. the wrong cage position, frequent disturbance, long journeys, or the wrong companions in a cage.

Unfortunately, even with the best of care, there may be setbacks, as Syrian hamsters of particular colours have an inherited susceptibility to certain illnesses. These genetically connected illnesses seem to be linked to the factor for patched fur and are identifiable by heightened nervousness.

Dwarf hamsters, given the right care, are less susceptible to illnesses, although, apparently, they may be more prone to liver and kidney ailments.

In principle, it is always advisable to consult a veterinarian or other expert because the risk of a wrong diagnosis, or of harming a hamster by giving it medicines intended for human beings, is high. Many pet-owners avoid going to the veterinarian because of the cost. Of course, the cost of treatment may be more than that of a replacement animal but so will that of the monthly food ration – and who would consider starving their pet for that reason? There is an obligation on an owner to seek proper advice for their pet when it is sick.

Symptoms of common illnesses

Diarrhoea can have many causes. Usually, an infection with bacteria, viruses or single-celled micro-organisms (protozoans) will develop if the animal is additionally weakened through adverse environmental conditions, e.g. bad or wrong food, or unclean litter. If the faeces are formless and smeary, but the hamster's behaviour is otherwise normal, immediately leave out the greenfood and juicy food. Give the animal weak, black tea or camomile tea (unsweetened!), crispbread and oats. If, in spite of this treatment, there is no improvement within 2–3 days, a serious infection is indicated that can only be treated by a veterinarian.

The result of a minor fight. These bite-wounds heal very quickly by themselves.

Respiratory ailments are indicated by clearly audible breathing, frequent sneezing and slightly sticky eyes. They may be caused by high humidity in the cage, draughts or sudden fluctuations in temperature. Remedy the causes and move the cage to a position where the temperature can be kept at about 23–25°C (73–77°F). If the symptoms do not improve after a few days, take your hamster to an animal clinic or an experienced veterinarian.

Small bites and other injuries usually heal up quite rapidly and present no problems. The animals will encourage the healing process

A close-up view of the four fingers of the front paws and the rudimentary thumb.

Above left: *Front paw.*
Above right: *Back paw with five toes.*

themselves by frequent licking. Human intervention, i.e. disinfecting or treating the wound, only rarely helps in the case of rodents.

With lack of supervision, or through negligence, a hamster may sometimes fall from a great height to the ground. Unfortunately, hamsters, unlike most other rodents which have longer tails, do not always land on their feet. Even if they do not sustain fatal injuries, they may appear to be dead – they may have received a shock from the fall. Place the animal back in its familiar cage and keep it warm. Observe it carefully. If it has not also sustained internal injuries, it will soon be running about again as before.

Internal injuries or broken bones are indicated by abnormal movements. Sadly, even a veterinarian will rarely be able to help. Trust in the hamster's own powers of healing, supported by doses of minerals and vitamins, or take your pet to a veterinary clinic.

Swellings, which can be seen or felt, sometimes form on different parts of the body. A swelling that enlarges very quickly may be a pus-filled abscess. This will usually burst open by itself. Abscesses are usually caused by small injuries in places which the hamster cannot lick clean. Treatment can be carried out by repeated dabbing and rinsing with mallow tea and camomile tea.

Gradually enlarging swellings, especially in older rodents, indicate malignant tumours (cancer). A vet can decide whether an operation would be reasonable. You may have to allow it to be put to sleep if it becomes apathetic and is suffering.

Problems with teeth may occur, particularly if the teeth used for gnawing are not naturally filed down constantly. This may be due to a lack of hard food or a deformation of the jaw. Unfortunately, the latter cannot be cured. The teeth will either have to be cut regularly by a veterinarian or the hamster will have to be put to sleep because teeth that are too long will make eating difficult or even impossible. Occasionally, the gnawing teeth may break off but if the hamster is given plenty of mineral compounds, they should quickly regrow.

Mites may be indicated by the presence of small fragments of skin. These parasites can cause loss of fur and badly itching patches, and the hamster's skin may become crusty and scaly. Although many rodents are known to be significant carriers of disease, and to harbour parasites, those bred by human beings experience surprisingly few problems in this respect.

Fungal skin infections have similar symptoms and can only be identified with certainty by a veterinarian.

Lymphochorionic meningitis (LCM) is an illness that only attacks hamsters up to the age of 3 months but it is fairly well known. The symptoms are not very distinctive but the illness can be transmitted to human beings. It is normally not very dangerous but may damage unborn human babies. Pregnant women should therefore avoid contact with hamsters younger than 3 months old.

Deficiencies can manifest themselves in a variety of ways but can be generally prevented by a balanced diet that includes vegetable and animal constituents. If the hamster is given a vitamin-rich diet many symptoms will disappear in a surprisingly short time.

Signs of old age will become apparent at the age of about 2– 2½ years, depending on the colour variety and species of the hamster. It will become apathetic, sleep far more than usual, eat less and move about with difficulty. It should be left in its usual surroundings and not taken out of its cage very often from this point onwards.

In the case of the Syrian hamster, the domestication process took place over several decades almost before our eyes. The current world-wide population of pet hamsters is now estimated at many millions.

A brief history of hamster-keeping

The Syrian, or golden, hamster (*Mesocricetus auratus*) was first described in 1839 by the naturalist G. R. Waterhouse. In 1930, Professor I. Aharoni, a zoologist from Jerusalem, managed to capture a small group of Syrian hamsters near Aleppo in Syria (where the first Syrian hamsters were found). In a deep burrow he found a mother with 12 young, of which only three survived. Soon, offspring were born to these young hamsters. Until very recently, all Syrian hamsters kept in captivity were descended from these few, closely related animals.

In 1938, hamsters arrived in the USA via the UK. After World War 2, Syrian hamsters were brought back to Europe because they were ideal animals for research. Shortly afterwards their comet-like

Facts and figures

	Syrian hamster	Chinese hamster	Russian and Roborovski's dwarf hamsters
Body mass	130–180 g	30–50 g	30–40 g
	(4⅝–6½ oz)	(1–1¾ oz)	(1–1½ oz) (20 g or ¾ oz)
Birth weight	1.5–2 g	1–1.5 g	1–1.5 g (less than 1/16 oz)
	(about 1/16 oz)	(less than 1/16 oz)	(0.8 g or less than 1/32 oz)
Gestation period	16–18 days	21 days	21 days
Maturity	30–50 days	30–40 days	30–50 days
Weaning age	22–25 days	20–25 days	21 days
Litter size	1–14	1–11	1–8 (1–6)
Litters per year	8–10	4–7	3–7
Life expectancy	2–3½ years	2–3½ years	2–3 years

rise to become one of the most popular domestic pets began. In spite of everything, strains have remained healthy and fertile.

The history of the dwarf hamsters is poorly documented in comparison, but the original stock of today's strains is certainly to be less closely related than that of the Syrian hamster.

The relatives of hamsters

A Chinese hamster.

Rodents, which comprise about 3,000 separate species, are the order of mammals with the most species. All hamsters belong to the suborder of mouse-related rodents (*Myomorpha*) and to the family of 'burrowers' (*Cricetidae*).

One of the best-known members of this group is the large **common hamster** (*Cricetus cricetus*), found throughout much of Europe and Asia. This most colourful of indigenous mammals is currently threatened with extinction in most parts of western Europe, in spite of its adaptability. It has therefore been protected in many countries, although this is not helping much, as the rate of change to the environment is ever-increasing. The habitat of this guinea-pig-sized rodent is fields and pastures. The use of massive amounts of pesticides and herbicides, combined with deep-ploughing, are driving away this animal, which was once regarded as a pest. For reasons of conservation and because of its size, we do not recommend keeping this very interesting and attractive rodent as a pet.

Apart from the **Syrian**, or **golden, hamster** (*Mesocricetus auratus*), three further species of the genus *Mesocricetus* are known, from Asia Minor, Bulgaria and Romania. These hamsters have almost never been available as domestic pets and, apart from some data on their distribution and biology, hardly anything is known about these closest relatives of the Syrian hamster.

A Russian dwarf hamster.

A similar situation prevails for several dwarf hamster species. One species of the genus *Cricetulus*, which also includes the Chinese hamster (*Cricetulus griseus*), has become distributed as far as Europe. The **migratory hamster** (*Cricetulus migratorius*) seems to be spreading and has even been observed, coming from Romania, at the southern tip of the Peloponnese in Greece. Some *Cricetulus* hamsters, e.g. *Cricetulus triton*, are unusual in having a relatively long tail.

Index

Picture sources
All photographs are by Regina Kuhn except that on page 46 (top) which is by Hans Reinhard. Black-and-white illustrations are by Siegfried Lokau, as specified by the author.

Acknowledgements
I would like to thank my parents, my brother Michi, Anja and Birgit Gollmann for their support. The hamsters photographed for this book were kindly supplied by Zoo-Kolle, of Stuttgart and Zoo-Utke, of Esslingen.

A BLANDFORD BOOK
First published in the UK 1997 by Blandford
A Cassell imprint
Cassell plc
Wellington House 125 Strand London WC2R 0BB

Text copyright © 1997 Cassell plc
Translated by Astrid Mick
Originally published as *Hamster* by Georg Gassner
World copyright © Eugen Ulmer GmbH & Co.,Stuttgart, Germany

All rights reserved. No part of this book may be reproduced or transmitted in any form or by any means, electronic or mechanical, including photocopying, recording or any information storage or retrieval system, without permission in writing from the copyright holder and publisher.

Distributed in the United States by Sterling Publishing Co., Inc.,
387 Park Avenue South, New York, NY 10016-8810

A Cataloguing-in-Publication Data entry for this title is available from the British Library

ISBN 0-7137-2680-6

Printed and bound in Spain